SELIM

THE HAT

BLOODAXE BOOKS

ISBN: 978 1 85224 806 2

First published 2008 by
Bloodaxe Books Ltd,
Highgreen,
Tarset,
Northumberland NE48 1RP.

www.bloodaxebooks.com
For further information about Bloodaxe titles
please visit our website or write to
the above address for a catalogue.

Bloodaxe Books Ltd acknowledges
the financial assistance of
Arts Council England, North East.

Cover design: Neil Astley & Pamela Robertson-Pearce.

Printed in Great Britain by
Bell & Bain Limited, Glasgow, Scotland.

CONTENTS

The Day the Cows Got Out

Oh my God, the cows have all got out,
but no one's taking any notice, are they,
they're looking for the father,
but he's gone,
and what's the mother doing down there? *Mother*,
mind out for those firemen everywhere,
pushing and shoving between the fire-engines,
and mind out for the cows;
and the heat!
(There shouldn't have been a baby in the first place –
it's far too late for that sort of thing…)
And here's the surgeon
with his lovely hands,
Oh dear, the baby's face is falling off
and her clothes are stuck to her skin, I'm afraid,
and all the tweezers in the world, Mother,
will never get them tweezered out again.
Easy does it, nurse, easy does it.
Drip that milk.
Bastard!
Easy does it.

Tortoise

She puts him in her bed
like a hand
that's never touched a human hand before,
a hand without an arm,
made of rock:
she takes it with her everywhere she goes!

Gentle Pressure on the Sides of Piglets

Gentle pressure on the sides of piglets
always makes them feel calmer, Mother;
and she herself is like a little piglet,
examining the graceful snails of Oxfordshire
and snuffling at their eyeless eyes and bellyfoots
and crushing them
(because she's *so* friendly!).

Peonies

She never sees the darkness of dark peonies
without the sense of being small and vigilant
coming quietly back to her again.

Goose

She's like a goose he stuffs with stuff like weights
that makes her feel so sick she can't refuse;
take this, he goes,
gag, gag, she goes,
and this –
and down it goes,
all this stuff she hates,
into the feathery throat: she's his
cold angel.

How Sweet the Voices

How sweet the voices of her uniform
that tell the world how innocent she is
but what she really is
they've no idea
or how the sunshine casts a long shadow
and how she lies like beans in a jar
lying with no hands in the shadow.

Heaven

Squashed beside her like a knee-length stallion
squashed inside a stall made of grunts,
this grunting man is surely much too close
for someone who's supposed to be in Heaven.

Sugar

She said
if he was dead he'd feel better –
either dead or down a long drive
in a huge Victorian building
with blocked windows
where nobody can see him
or hear him
or fear the darkness of his sugary ways.
Sugar, sugar, sugar. White grains.

Being Warm is Nice

She's like a little snowball!
And, like snowballs,
she doesn't like to feel she's getting warm –
but *being warm is nice!*
She needs to know that,
it means you can be swallowed after all!

Corsetry

Oh my God,
this girl needs holding together,
send her something, God,
if only corsetry,
whose warm elastic fingers hold on *tight*,
like God might hold her,
but He's got no fingers.

Lily and Beef

He's burnt her swimsuit.
Funny, isn't he?
One breast is white,
the other one's gone red.
Lily and Beef, he calls them. Very funny.
(This is just between ourselves, OK.)

Stories about Horses

Supper on a tray in the drawing-room
and nothing said.
Or if they do say anything
they like to tell her stories about horses.
Every night the sky is full of horses.
She goes to sleep with horses round her neck.

The Darkness of Her Meekness

She rages in the darkness of the meekness
in which they have installed her as in stalls
while in the lounge her mother and her sisters
further their spectacular depressions.

Turpentine

The man who burns her burns her all the time.
Why?
Because he loves her!
Yes, that's right:
he loves her hair,
he loves her lovely thighs,
he loves the way she lies there like a lump
breathing in the smell of her own singeing.
O come and sit beside her while she sleeps!
Close her eyes and let her smell your arm!
The man who burns her
smells of turpentine
that penetrates his sandwiches and bandages
and makes her wish she knew
those secret things
other women cheerfully call *nothing*.

King of Trout

His body, like a partly-jewelled trout,
doesn't make a sound. Thank God for that!

The Sort of Neck People Want to Strangle

Can't you see your daughter's snowy neck's
the sort of neck people want to strangle?
Can't you see the way
it's *asking for it* –
sweet but nasty, Mother?
Yes, she can.

Her Wheezy Mother

Her wheezy mother dresses her in dresses
made of thistles, artichokes and porcupines –
like somebody might dress her
who is sick,
and isn't now,
and never was,
her mother.

Pain

She only wants the kind of pain she wants
and not the kind of pain she feels here,
crushed between the standard lamps and lampshades
and switches and flexes and chains.

Gold Snails

Women are like gardens where gold snails
are walking back and forth in the rain
and as they walk their curious long feet
are feeling for a surface to console them.

Bicycle

Her mother's found her someone she can *lean on* –
as if she were a bicycle!
How dare she!
As if she were a sparkly married bicycle
which wouldn't dream of being mainly throat;
which wouldn't dream of being eased open
and being used as someone else's throat.

The Holy Brains of Snails

Deep within the glades of giant rhubarb leaves
the holy brains of snails worship moistness
and down among the roots in the river
the lanky froglets worship moistened mud
and underneath her eiderdowns our heroine
is busily worshipping herself.
(She's under the impressions that it's God
who's loving her so much
but it's herself!)

Aeroplane

Her husband lies beside her like an aeroplane
lying on its side in a wood
whose body is encrusted with gold snails
that used to grace the mouths of billionaires.

Penetrative Sex and Housewifery

Although she doesn't know what it is
she knows this isn't it.
She's not stupid!
She prays to God.
She struggles to explain.
Penetrative sex and housewifery
do not really interest her that much.

Footwear

Men kill each other as and when they can
and when they can't they *do each other's heads in*
and women with red knickers and red nails
and red high-heeled footwear are to blame.

Articulate Serrations

Articulate serrations of cracked skulls
tell us God
has been here before us,
or something has,
and might come again –
something with a little spade or scalpel
whose blades are rays
and know the darkness needs them.

A Noisy Horse

He's lost inside the tunnels of her hair
where nothing can be seen except a jaw
and nothing can be heard except a horse
chewing carrots with its beige teeth.

Snow

He drags his heavy limbs across her body
like something dead dragged across snow,
rutted snow;
it's lust that does the dragging
across a wife encased in ice and snow.

Semolina

This person ought to do as she is told
and not come snooping into private offices
where chairs and tables dream the private dreams
that even now advance towards a dress
that's closing over them like semolina!

Glass

Her mouth is like a mouth dipped in glass –
and no one likes to lick or chew glass!

Inside Her Hat

Can we ask a simple question? *No.*
We only want to help her! *No, no, no.*
Nothing we can say can reach the ears
curled up tight inside her hat like watches.

Suitcases

A million squeaky suitcases on wheels
are being dragged about inside her head
and every time she asks them to *pipe down*
the tiny wheels squeak at her some more.

Going Shopping

Today she has decided to go shopping.
It's not much fun stuck at home, is it?
Look at all those heavy bags of hers!
They huddle at her feet like ducks and geese
waiting dimly for their new home.

Happiness

He sees her painted nails and he knows
that *everything is about to change*:
she's happy, happy, happy, like the Danes
who get so happy that they kill themselves!
(I don't know how to say this but alas
in her dreams she makes him eat kaka.)

What She Really Wants

What she really wants is a desert
where wild horses break the speed of sound
and where a man is hurrying towards her
who only ever wants to play the piano.

Goose Feathers

God has got a larder full of angels
gripping geese
between their huge thighs
and as they pluck and pluck
she feels feathers
settle on her skin:
she can't stand it!

Violence

Her heart is like a room full of roses
that fall apart
like dry white wounds;
her heart is like a garden full of wounds
that know that pain
needs them and aches for them,
like mothers
whose stiff nipples
ache for mouths,
and cast around for them violently.

Love Ah Love

Love?
Ah, love
is like a veil round her,
and, as the years go by,
many veils,
and sometimes she can't see,
and some kind person
will leave the crowd
and come and hold her hand.

The Sun Is Beating Down

The sun is beating down on Arizona,
it blinds the yellow eyes of the colts,
it coats the sandy cottonwood in silver
and everywhere it goes
it hears your boots.

The Tiny Room

Her tiny room is chock-a-block with crockery
and leatherware and hosiery and saddlery
and God Himself with all His horsey angels
is actually unable to get through to her!

The Cloudless Skies of Texas

Anyway she doesn't want this room.
This pokey little room.
She wants Texas.
She wants to hit the cloudless skies of Texas
and Texas after Texas after Texas
(although she knows f-all about Texas
except that men on horses ride across it!).

Tomato Dreamer

This woman's so in love she can't stand it!
She loves you like a dream made of blood,
she loves you like tomatoes in white milk
that never asks them not to be so red;
she loves you like a furious little strawberry
sinking down into a snowdrop wood.

When God Is on His Horse

Touch her
and she blinks
like the sun
when God is on His horse in Arizona.

Loves Falls Like Snow

Love falls like snow
in which a tall rider
is biting women
with his stout teeth
as if it's something
riders always do
when actually what they like is singing!

Out Beyond the Sandy Pines

Out beyond the sandy pines, Mother,
where lovers are half-human and half-hare,
a sandy man is cradling your daughter
who offers him a choice of burnt hollows.

Paradise Is Leather

Paradise is leather in Wyoming
where wild horses gallop up and down
and every day the yellow sun goes nuts
and teeny flies make love and spread diseases.

Gold Cup

Underneath her bra her little heart
is racing like a racer in a race
that never stops to think about what happened
on other days
that have been and gone.

It Was the Size of a Pea

Once it was the size of a ballroom
where fillies gather to enjoy the night,
their floor-length manes and tails swirling wildly,
but first it was the size of a pea.
Various other sizes happened later,
including ones as big and fat as hot-house plants
that grow to be the size of Arizona
but first it was the size of a pea.

Rock

On slabs of rock
man-sized birds call home,
rows of women
fry themselves like chops
but by the afternoon
they'll be sobbing.

Women Without Men

Women without men are the worst:
they smell of fish,
their eyes are red from crying,
and if and when they come
they come like puddings!

Necklaces and Chains

You crunch across the gravel like a bear
glittering with necklaces and chains –
tinkle tinkle crunch, tinkle crunch! –
but when you say hello
she practically faints.

Think of It As Mooing

Think of it as mooing.
She's a cow
who never thinks of God without mooing –
a lovely milky sound
which sounds like love
if love were made of milk
and liked mooing.

The River

Let's leave them by the looping golden river
where God has found his way into each goose;
or, if there are no geese by the river,
and if there are some ducks, then each duck.

God Has Found His Way into Each Duck

God has found his way into each duck,
each snow-white lily, each be-jewelled trout;
each wheezy little mother, wheezy father,
each creaker of each granulated boot,
God has found His way into Wyoming,
Arizona, Texas, Tennessee,
and everywhere she doesn't know the name of,
and obviously everywhere He does
(and everywhere He goes He takes His horse
and strokes its nose) and into every stork.

Hands of Mercy, Hands of Caramel

How beautiful you are,
how like a burrow
in whose enormous hands she lies sleeping,
hands of mercy,
hands of caramel,
if caramel could rock her
and could sing.

Selima Hill grew up in a family of painters in farms in England and Wales, and has lived in Dorset for the past 20 years. She won first prize in the Arvon/*Observer* International Poetry Competition with part of *The Accumulation of Small Acts of Kindness* (1989), one of several extended sequences in *Gloria: Selected Poems* (Bloodaxe Books, 2008). Published at the same time as her new collection, *The Hat* (2008), *Gloria* includes work from *Saying Hello at the Station* (1984), *My Darling Camel* (1988), *A Little Book of Meat* (1993), *Aeroplanes of the World* (1994), *Violet* (1997), *Bunny* (2001), *Portrait of My Lover as a Horse* (2002), *Lou-Lou* (2004) and *Red Roses* (2006).

Violet was a Poetry Book Society Choice and was shortlisted for all three of the UK's major poetry prizes, the For-ward Prize, T.S. Eliot Prize and Whitbread Poetry Award. *Bunny* won the Whitbread Poetry Award, was a Poetry Book Society Choice and was also shortlisted for the T.S. Eliot Prize. *Lou-Lou* was a Poetry Book Society Recommendation. She was given a Cholmondeley Award in 1986, and was a Royal Literary Fund Fellow at the University of Exeter in 2003-06.

Selima Hill reads a half-hour selection of her poems on *The Poetry Quartets: 2* (Bloodaxe Books/The British Council, 1998), a double-cassette shared with Fleur Adcock, Carol Ann Duffy and Carol Rumens.

As a tutor, Selima Hill has worked in prisons, hospitals and monasteries as well as for the Arvon Foundation and London's South Bank Centre. She has worked on several collaborations with artists including: *Parched Swallows* with choreographer Emily Claid; *Point of Entry* with sculptor Bill Woodrow; and *Trembling Hearts in the Bodies of Rocks* with performance artist Ilona Medved-Lost.